RUBY - ru·by (roo-bee):
1: a jewel, a precious
   stone that is red.

BRIDGES - bridg·es (brij-ez):
Plural of Bridge
1a: a structure carrying
    a pathway or roadway
    over an obstacle
    (such as a river).
1b: a time, place, or
    means of connection
    or transition.

To Lucille, Dick, and Bernette, who are in their own special way
partly responsible for *I Am Ruby Bridges*.
May they rest in God's Perfect Peace! **—R.B.**

To every child who was told that they do not belong. **—N.S.**

Text copyright © 2022 by Ruby Bridges
Illustrations copyright © 2022 by Nikkolas Smith

Photos © : Back Cover: Slade Paul / Getty Images

Library of Congress Cataloging-in-Publication Number: 2021042308

ISBN 978-1-338-75388-2

10 9 8 7 6 5 4 3 2 1   22 23 24 25 26

Printed in China   62
First edition, September 2022

Book design by Rae Crawford

I Am
Ruby Bridges

written by **Ruby Bridges**
art by **Nikkolas Smith**

Orchard Books
an imprint of Scholastic Inc. • New York

I am Ruby Bridges.
When I grow up, my work will be **precious**,
I will be a bridge . . .

I will bridge the "gap" between Black and white . . .
. . . and hopefully between all people.

I suppose some things in life
are just meant to be.

1960

Before I started school, I wasn't thinking about who I would be
when I grew up.
What I was thinking about was how much I didn't even *like* my name.
I thought "Ruby" was a name for little old ladies.
It was much too old for someone my age.
After all, I was only just turning six.

I'm told my grandmother chose this name, Ruby, for me.
Well, that explains it!
No wonder it's such an **ancient** name.

But I so loved my grandmother,
I thought *I'll just have to live with it
and try to grow into it!*
Surely, I didn't want to hurt her feelings.

So there I was, almost six,
born in 1954.
I'm told that was a very important year
because of the **landmark case**: *Brown v. Board of Education*!
That was when the court banned segregation in schools.

But all I knew then was my old name was Ruby Bridges.
OH BOY! What's next?
What a way to start school!

Oh well, how bad can it be? I thought.
It's not like I'll be the first Ruby
in the world, just the youngest one.

So, off to school I go.

JOHNSON LOCKETT
PUBLIC SCHOOL

It is a regular school with lots of other kids to play with.
I make new best friends, even my teacher is nice,
and it's not hard at all!
Surprisingly, it's easier than I thought it would be.
I get lots of gold stars every day.
Life couldn't be better.

HARRIET
FANNIE
WHITNEY
MALCOLM
MEDGAR
MARTIN
RUBY

Then, just as things are going really well for me, **SURPRISE!**
I find out my parents have decided I am switching schools.
"To a better school," they say. "With better opportunities."
But first, I must take a test to get in.

OPPORTUNITIES

What are opportunities anyway?
I thought. And why do I need them?
Especially if a test comes with them!

But then I thought *I'm already getting gold stars,*
so how hard can it be?
Besides, there is no turning back now.
It's what my parents want for me.

OPPORTUNITIES

And guess what?
Another gold star!
I passed the test.

Can you believe it?
How lucky can an almost six-year-old with
an old name like Ruby be?
I was about to find out,
because my mom said I would be starting at a brand new school
the next morning and I had better behave!

First Day

No more walking to school with my best friends.
There are four very tall men at the door
to drive me to school. And they're white men.
Who in the world are they?
And who told them I needed a ride to school anyway?

Federal marshals, they tell me —
sent by the president of the United States.

Federal marshals sent just for me?
WOW!
That must have been a very special test
that I passed, because they said I'm
"THE FIRST."

The first what? I thought.
I didn't find out what being "the first" *really* meant
until the day I arrived at this new school.

Those four very tall white men? They **escort** me into the building past lots of screaming white people who line the streets outside the school. It really looks like **Mardi Gras** to me, but they aren't throwing any beads. What's Mardi Gras without beads?

U.S. MAI

AL

Once I get inside,
I meet the new principal,
and she is white, too.

I wasn't taken to my new classroom
until the next day.

Second Day

When I arrive at my classroom, my new
teacher opens the door and greets me.

"Hi, I'm Mrs. Henry, your teacher.
Come in and take a seat," she says.
And aren't I surprised.
Because she is also white.
I never had a white teacher before.

And the biggest surprise of all?
I am the only kid in the class.
I didn't see any other kids at all.
Not one.

That test must have been a lot harder than I thought.

Why am I the only kid in my class?
Not to mention the only kid in the whole school.
And why don't I see anyone who looks like me?

And then that's when it hits me.

I am not just the *only kid*, I'm the only Black person here.
I thought: *Maybe I am the first!*

W. FRANTZ ELEMENTARY
CLASS PHOTOS

1930s

1940s

1950s

1960

The first Black kid in this school.
So *that's* what they meant about me being the first.

Finally, it all makes sense.
Me, six-year-old Ruby!
The first Black kid to go to this school,
William Frantz Elementary.
A white school.

When I asked my mom, she said, "Yes. It *was* an all-white school, until the **laws** changed — when *Brown v. Board of Education* won their case in the **Supreme Court**."

Now all Black kids can go to any school they like alongside white kids.

I, Ruby, being the first, helped to make that possible.

And that's a good thing, for Black kids. For white kids, too . . .

. . . for all kids once they finally get here!

I just want to know one thing . . .
When are they coming?
Because I know they are just like me.
Who cares what colors we are?
I'm just happy *Brown v. Board* made it right.
School is just school and kids are just kids.

I'm sure they'll all show up soon enough.
I can't wait!

I guess being six
with an old name like Ruby
isn't so bad after all.

I suppose some things in life ARE meant to be!

I am Ruby Bridges.
The first!

Glossary

ancient an·cient *(**ayn**-shuhnt)* adjective
Very old.

Brown v. Board of Education noun
A landmark court case in 1954. The Supreme Court decided that public schools should not be segregated.

case case *(kase)* noun
A trial in a court of law.

escort es·cort *(i-**skort**)* verb
To go with or follow someone, especially for protection, as in a police escort.

federal fed·er·al *(**fed**-ur-uhl)* adjective
In a country with a federal government, such as the United States, several states are united under and controlled by one central power or authority. However, each state also has its own government and can make its own laws.

landmark land·mark *(**land**-mahrk)* noun
An important event.

law law *(law)* noun
A rule established and enforced by a government.

Mardi Gras noun
A festival that takes place on the Tuesday before Ash Wednesday. One of the more famous celebrations takes place in New Orleans, Louisiana.

marshal mar·shal *(**mahr**-shuhl)* noun
A police officer who is responsible for a particular area.

opportunity op·por·tu·ni·ty *(ah-pur-**too**-ni-tee)* noun
A chance or a good time to do something. *(plural: opportunities)*

precious pre·cious *(**presh**-uhs)* adjective
(1) Very valuable, as in a precious gem, (2) Very special or dear, as in a precious child.

president pres·i·dent *(**prez**-i-duhnt)* noun
The elected leader or chief executive of a republic.

Supreme Court noun
The highest and most powerful court in the United States. It has the power to overturn decisions made in lower courts and also to declare laws unconstitutional.

United States noun
A country in North America established in 1776.

Author's Note

As I began writing I AM RUBY BRIDGES, I knew I wanted to unfold a different version of my story. One that was told from my own six-year-old self and met picture book readers eye-to-eye. I wanted to invite young readers today to probe deeper and offer them a new window into another morsel of history. My goal was to captivate these curious minds while teaching them about a very important moment and time in our history. A moment that changed the face of education in our country.

I naturally leaned toward the sense of humor of a child. I thought back to my own sense of humor as a six-year-old. And voilà! Out of the mouths of babes, this version was born!

Here, I invite readers to journey back with me to the time when I was five and then six years old, when I didn't quite know who I was or who I wanted to be when I grew up. Most of us at that time had no idea where our names originated. I wanted to create a space for young children to read my story from the perspective of me as a child. I hope they discover I was not much different from them. I was inquisitive, creative, and inquiring, just like them.

In my story, you will notice that I include a glossary, another tool to help young readers expand their vocabulary, to connect their imagination to learning. Words are highlighted in "Ruby" red.

Finally, I must mention the illustrations. Oh my! They allow readers to take a colorful, lively journey with me. What a trip this will be!

—Ruby Bridges

Illustrator's Note

Growing up seeing Norman Rockwell's Ruby Bridges painting on the wall of my home, and being one of the few Black faces in my elementary school in Texas, I knew that she was a huge reason why there was any progress at all.

It is an immense honor to now have the opportunity to illustrate Ms. Ruby's picture book. As I began to visually develop the artwork for this project, hearing Ms. Ruby's firsthand account of this historic time in her life helped me realize how colorfully vibrant hope and optimism should appear through her six-year-old eyes. To ask, what did her opportunities look like? To inspire you all to envision: What do your opportunities look like?

The artwork in this book was also created to encourage you to keep the vision of a more connected human race alive in your minds at all times. I explored how I could visually represent young Ruby as a bridge, being such an iconic connector of people when our country needed it desperately. May this book be a reminder that even if racism never goes away completely, we must always stand fearless against it in our search for justice and equality.

—Nikkolas Smith

i am special...

i can be President...
(and vice president!)

i am precious...

i have opportunities...

i am Ruby... the first!